Oxford University Press, Great Clarendon Street, Oxford OX2 6DP

Oxford   New York
Athens   Auckland   Bangkok   Bogota   Bombay
Buenos Aires   Calcutta   Cape Town   Dar es Salaam   Delhi
Florence   Hong Kong   Istanbul   Karachi
Kuala Lumpur   Madras   Madrid   Melbourne
Mexico City   Nairobi   Paris   Singapore
Taipei   Tokyo   Toronto   Warsaw

and associated companies in
Berlin   Ibadan

Oxford is a trade mark of Oxford University Press

Illustrations © Nick Sharratt 1998
Arrangement and Selection © Jill Bennett 1998

A CIP catalogue record for this book is available
from the British Library

ISBN 0 19 276173 0 (hardback)
ISBN 0 19 276174 9 (paperback)

**In memory of George and Winifred Davison
– NS**

**For Daisy, Dilpreet, Harry, Louise, Owen,
Priya, Rachel, Sadiq, Sumeera, Taranjit,
and Mary el Jamal
– JB**

Acknowledgements

The editor and publisher are grateful for permission to
include the following poems:

Ashley Bryan: 'Rain coming' reprinted from Sing to the
Sun, Copyright © 1992 by Ashley Bryan, by permission of
HarperCollins Publishers (USA).

Michael Harrison: 'On the beach' reprinted from Junk Mail
by Michael Harrison (OUP, 1993), by permission of the
author.

Richard Edwards: 'Mermaid' reprinted from If Only . . .
(Viking, 1990), by permission of the author.

Florence Parry Heide: 'Rocks' reprinted from Poems
Children Will Sit Still For (Scholastic, Inc), by permission of
the author.

Wes Magee: 'The Harbour Wall', reprinted by permission
of the author.

Margaret Mahy: 'Goodness Gracious' reprinted from The
First Margaret Mahy Storybook (Dent 1972), by permission
of the Orion Publishing Group Ltd.

Robin Mellor: 'Whale Dance', Copyright © Robin Mellor
1998, first published here by permission of the author.

Judith Nicholls: 'Picnic' reprinted from Wish You Were
Here (OUP, 1992), by permission of the author; 'Oh, dizzy
Me' and 'Let's do the flip-flop frolic!', both Copyright ©
Judith Nicholls 1998, first published here by permission of
the author.

Telcine Turner: 'Listen' reprinted from Song of the Surreys
(Macmillan Caribbean, 1977), by permission of the author.

Valerie Worth: 'Starfish' reprinted from All the Small Poems
and Fourteen More, Copyright © 1987, 1994 by Valerie
Worth, by permission of Farrar, Straus & Giroux, Inc.

SEASIDE POEMS

Collected by Jill Bennett
Illustrated by Nick Sharratt

Oxford University Press

Let's do the flip-flop frolic!

Pop on a flip-flop,
flip on a plop-plip,
flop on a plip-plop,
flick on a flop-flip,

and . . .

hop-along
pop-along
flounce-along
bounce-along
prance-along
dance-along

into

the

. . .

SPLASH!

Judith Nicholls

Goodness gracious!

Goodness gracious, fiddle dee dee!
Somebody's grandmother out at sea!

Just where the breakers begin to bound
Somebody's grandmother bobbing around.

Up on the shore the people shout,
'Give us a hand and we'll pull you out!'

'No!' says the granny. 'I'm right as rain,
And I'm going to go on till I get to Spain.'

Margaret Mahy

Picnic

George, lend a hand
and spread that cloth,
the sand is everywhere!
Just look at that,
you'd never think
it took hours to prepare!

WAKE UP, GRAMP!
Your food's all out,
get it while you can!
Have a lemonade before
it warms up in the sun.

What is it, Mum?

There's . . .

ham with sand,
and spam with sand,
there's chicken paste
and lamb with sand;
oranges, bananas,
lemonade or tea;
bread with sand
all spread with sand —
at least the sand comes free!
We've crisps with sand
and cake with sand —
it's grand with lunch or tea —
crunch it up,
enjoy it, love,
at least we're by the sea!

Judith Nicholls

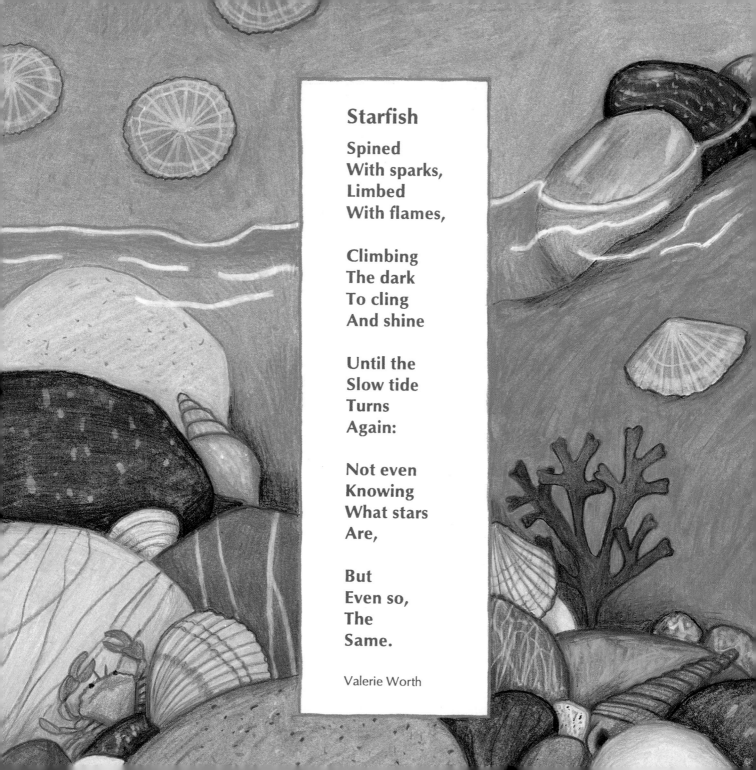

Starfish

Spined
With sparks,
Limbed
With flames,

Climbing
The dark
To cling
And shine

Until the
Slow tide
Turns
Again:

Not even
Knowing
What stars
Are,

But
Even so,
The
Same.

Valerie Worth

Rocks

Big rocks into pebbles,
pebbles into sand.
I really hold a million million rocks here in my hand.

Florence Parry Heide

On the beach

The waves claw
At the shingle
Time after time.
They fall back
Again and again,
Sighing, sighing.

Michael Harrison

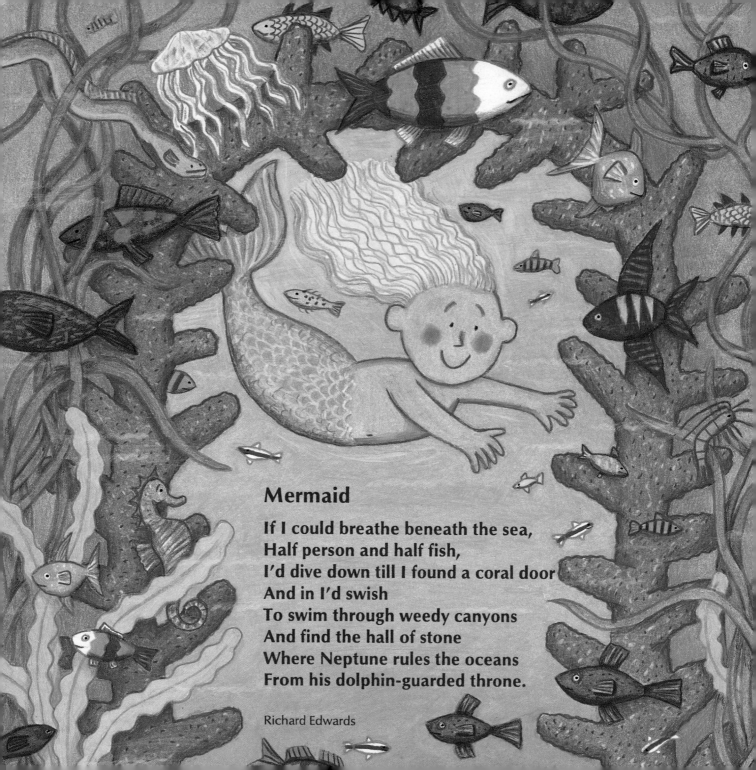

Mermaid

If I could breathe beneath the sea,
Half person and half fish,
I'd dive down till I found a coral door
And in I'd swish
To swim through weedy canyons
And find the hall of stone
Where Neptune rules the oceans
From his dolphin-guarded throne.

Richard Edwards

Rain coming

When a mermaid winks
Look for a shower
Children at the seashore
Splashing by the hour
See rain coming
Soaked as they can get
Cry, 'Quick!
Duck under
So you don't get wet!'

Ashley Bryan

Listen

Shhhhhhhhh!
Sit still, very still
And listen.
Listen to wings
Lighter than eyelashes
Stroking the air.
Know what the thin breeze
Whispers on high
To the coconut trees.
Listen and hear.

Telcine Turner

Oh, dizzy me!

STOP, let me off!
I squirm and squeal . . .
but I love to twirl and roll
on the fun-fair wheel!

Judith Nicholls

The harbour wall

In winter
when the wind blows wild
and the sea's as grey
as a muddy puddle,

the harbour wall
curls its long arm
around the boats
bobbing in a huddle.

'I'll keep you safe,'
the wall seems to say.
'Come here.' And it gives
the boats a cuddle.

Wes Magee

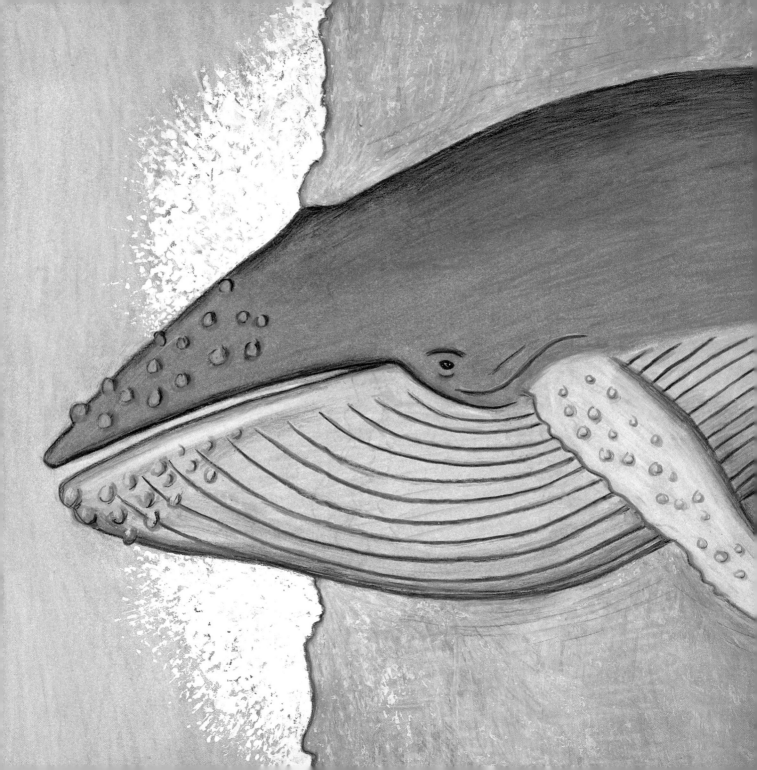

Whale-dance

Far out on an icy grey sea,
where daylight shines so pale,
the water is white, at the site
of the dance of the Hump-Back Whale.

Like monsters in the white foam
they stand on broad blue tails,
and while we sleep, they dive deep
in the dance of the Hump-Back Whale.

When we wake up in the morning
and wish we had a boat to sail,
the music in our ears, seems very near,
from the dance of the Hump-Back Whale.

Robin Mellor